BYGONE LEEK

THE 20TH CENTURY IN PHOTOGRAPHS

Cathryn Walton & Lindsey Porter

Published by
Guidelines Books & Sales
11 Belmont Road, Ipstones, Stoke on Trent ST10 2JN
Tel: 07971 990 649
Email: author.porter@gmail.com

ISBN: 978-1-84306-419-0

Print: Berforts Information Press, Eynsham, Oxford
Design: Michelle Prost

Front cover: VE Day 1945, Sheepmarket.
Back cover Top: High Street.
Back cover Bottom Left: West Street Sunday School Scholars head to the Market Place in 1910.
Back cover Bottom Right: An errand boy in his white apron waits for his orders in the Market Place.
Page 3: Challinor Fountain in the Market Place

BYGONE LEEK

THE 20TH CENTURY IN PHOTOGRAPHS

Cathryn Walton & Lindsey Porter

Contents

An early view of the Market Place before the Buttermarket was built in 1897. The two small shops next to the Red Lion were occupied by George Allen, a saddler and harness maker, and by the Hassall family whose daughter Ellen traded as a milliner. Woolworths has been established on the ground floor of the former Blacks Head since 1931, when it opened as a fancy bazaar. Built to a design by William Sugden in the late 1850's the new Blacks Head replaced an earlier inn of the same name. Boards on the front of the inn carry the name of Mr Lowe, a wine merchant, who is advertising Guinness and stout.

The stately Georgian house, home to the Cruso family, looks out over a deserted Market Place, stacked with stalls. Howe's grocers shop can be seen to the right as can a woollen drapers whose name appears to be Garside. Howe's was a family business, Thomas Howe passed on the business to his son Samuel.

Men, women, children, horses, handcarts, trestles, canopies, stalls and shops combine to paint a picture of another bustling Market Day in the early years of the century. An eager vendor brings forward his wares in a pony and trap while a carriage and horses await passengers outside the Red Lion.

An errand boy in his white apron waits for his orders; rabbits and hens in cages stand on the stones waiting to be sold. One of Leek's old gas lamps can be seen in front of the Challinor fountain.

This photograph taken before 1889 shows the old Bird in Hand, Redfern's baby linen shop, Warren's boot and shoe warehouse and William Henry Middleton's grocers shop. Sheets have been hung over the windows to protect goods from the sun. The shop between Redfern's and Warren's is probably that of John Adams who was a draper. The arch by the side of the shop led to Adam's Yard which held two houses.

The same shops in the 1960's. T.H. Booth, leather factors, now occupy the premises shared by Warren's shoe warehouse and Middleton's shop in the above photograph. In former years Thomas Henry Booth, tanner, currier and leather merchant, had a shop at 10, St. Edward Street and a tannery at 46, Ball Haye Road. Customers buying their nails from Booth's earlier this century would find they were wrapped in twists of paper taken from children's handwriting books! 21 and 22 Market Place have housed many shops over the years including Fitelson's Bazaar; today they are occupied by Oxfam. Next door is Beverley's wine and spirit merchants trading from the shop which was once John Adams drapers shop. Another charity shop has taken over this building, namely Imperial Cancer Research.

Micah Carding traded as a painter, plumber and glazier at 2 and 3 Market Place for many years. Carding's shop was part of the former Cock Inn, a flourishing establishment in the 18th century, able to provide numerous beds for weary travellers and several private parlours for exclusive use. In 1731 John Naden spent his last night in the cellars of the Cock before he was hung on Gun and his corpse gibbeted there. In later years part of these premises were used as a bank. In 1864 the inn was purchased by the Leek Improvement Commissioners who were considering building a new Town Hall and a covered market on the site. At this time the old inn had been divided into two shops, (pictured above) a doctors surgery, a blacksmith's shop, a cottage and several storerooms. The shops faced the Market Place but the other premises fronted Stockwell Street.

This large property was demolished and new premises built which house the Tourist Information Centre and council offices.

The Earl of Shrewsbury's coach waits patiently for a dog to cross over the cobbles in 1893. Between Carding's and the Red Lion are Henry Ellerton's drapers shop and George Lee Baskerville's watch and clock makers shop. Just visible on the left is the sign over Nathan Gosling's shop. He was a clothier and tailor. The Earl sold the horses in October 1893. Was this a photo of his last coach service between Alton Towers and Buxton?

Built by Thomas Joliffe, a wool merchant in 1627, this building was the Hall House. The exact date when it became the Red Lion is not known, although Joliffe sold his Staffordshire estate in 1765. In the early 19th century as many as 1,000 people would attend the Court leet held in the Red Lion Inn by the Earl of Macclesfield's steward. No doubt the event was good for socialising too. When balls were held in the Assembly Room the Market Place would be crowded with people anxious to glimpse the finery and feathers of ladies alighting from their carriages.

Young ladies would be equally keen to catch the eye of officers, in their colourful uniforms, who used the Red Lion as a 'mess' when troops passed through the town. On a more sombre note, a tragedy occurred here in 1836 when a traveller from Brazil shot himself shortly after leaving the 'Defiance' stagecoach.

When Mr Swift was the landlord in the early 1900s the family couch in the coffee room was upholstered with the hair of their pet pony whose tail hung from the centre of the seat at the end! In more recent years dinners and dances have been held here, travellers have been accommodated and townsfolk have

quenched their thirst at the bar. After a period of neglect, the Red Lion has emerged from its dilapidated hibernation and is once again a popular social centre for the people of Leek.

The rear of the Red Lion with a cart and carriage standing on the cobbled Red Lion yard.

William Sugden was the architect of the Black's Head at the bottom of the Market Place in the late-1850s. It replaced an earlier half-timbered inn of the same name sometimes called the Blackamoors Head. Woolworth's is now established on the ground floor of this former inn.

A local defence volunteer service was formed in May 1940 and soon received over 600 applications from local men. Although the age limits were 17 to 65, many applications were received from boys under 17, the oldest applicant being 70! Here the assembled ranks of the Leek Home Guard, as they were named, are ready to be inspected by the Earl of Harrowby in October 1940.

Right: This is the old Town Hall situated at the bottom of Leek Market Place, built in 1806 at a cost of £808.17s.5d. No longer suitable for a town the size of Leek it had become obsolete and was auctioned off in 1872. It was purchased by Joseph Flower with a bid of £85 and transported to Rosebank Street and used in the building of Portland House.

What are little boys made of? Bashful smiles, cheeky grins, resignation, boredom and bravado feature on these faces of boys taking part in Club Day c.1930. After all what young boy wants to be dressed in his best and walk around with girls!

Girls from St. John's Sunday School hold on to their ribbons as they assemble in the Market Place in the 1940s.

With well scrubbed knees, slicked down hair and beaming smiles these young lads prepare to sing lustily in the Market Place c.1958.

Sunday School teachers, banner bearers and pupils from St.Luke's captured on film in the mid 1950s. The man holding the banner is John Spilsbury.

Club Day in the 1970s. The Market Place is not nearly as crowded as it was in former years and there is definitely not so many hats!

Seen here is Pickford's grocers shop on the corner of St. Edward Street and High Street. The premises were built in 1907 for Mr. Ernie Green who kept a shop on the opposite corner. The Pickford family traded here for many years until Kevin Pickford and his wife, Stella, closed the shop in 2000. Nowadays it is a carpet shop. The shop next to Pickford's was once Pegg's green grocers, then a bookshop and now sells fabrics. The next three properties were demolished to make way for the new General Post Office which opened in 1964.

This street scene from the 1960s shows Westminster Bank on the corner of High Street with the Wilkes' Head public house next door. Above the entrance to Court No.2 is Stannard's shoe shop followed by Norman Ash's jewellery shop. Parr's bank was built on the site of the old Plough Inn in 1885. This was a Warrington based business and not surprisingly the bank in Leek was built to a design by W. Owen of Warrington. By 1923, the bank had become the Westminster Bank Ltd. The bank on this site closed in 1970 and the premises are now used by Leek Volunteer Bureau.

The Wilkes Head is one of only five inns in Britain named after the political reformer. Parker's brewery which provided the beer for this pub was taken over by Ind Coope. Stannard's shoe shop is now the home of the John Worthy Gallery while Norman Ash's shop is occupied by Go-Go Designs.

The Globe Inn in St. Edward Street, which was demolished to make way for the entrance to High Street. It stood just below the junction with Sheepmarket and was only an inn for about 75 years. This old stone house had previously been the home of a number of Leek silk manufacturers. Behind the inn, in the Globe Yard stood a warehouse and workshop which was formerly a silk shade or factory. Part of these premises can still be seen behind the façade of the travel agents in High Street. Cathryn Walton's great-great-great grandfather was once the innkeeper here and was fined for watering down his spirits!

Leek's first purpose built Post Office stood on the corner of Strangman Street and St. Edward Street. This interesting building opened in or shortly after 1905; with its decorative brickwork and elegant stonework this Post Office was certainly more pleasing to the eye than its replacement further up the street. A new telephone exchange opened in the Post Office yard in 1928. In 1968, a subscriber trunk dialling exchange was built on the site of this old Post Office.

Soldiers stand in line outside the shop of Mottershead and Son who were watchmakers trading from 41 St Edward Street in the early 20th century. Today the staff of Spruce and Dapper offers haircuts and male grooming from this shop.

The street decorated ready for the coronation festivities in 1911. The young lady in the pushchair gazes at the fluttering flags while the gentleman in the bowler hat seems to be studying his hand! Ladies stroll serenely, errand boys pause pensively while delivering bread and carrier's carts clatter over the cobbles. Gas lamps guard the wide pavements and railings protect the fronts of the "gentlemens' residences" to the left of the street.

This unique photograph shows the Quiet Woman and the Unicorn before 1897. In that year the Unicorn was set back and rebuilt and the workmen can be seen preparing to start some sort of renovation. For many years John Benson was the landlord of the Unicorn at the same time being landlord of the Talbot and the Sea Lion.

In 1793 the Quiet Woman was called the Good Woman, but before that date it was the White Hart. The Quiet

and Good elements of the name refer to the fact that the lady in question had no head and so could not talk! An example of early sexism! An old rhyme reads:-

"Here you may find a good woman
Faithfully portrayed from ye life
Nothing is wanting but her head
Because that turns with every wind
If the head had been left her
She would never have been good in all her life"

The old inn sign portrayed a headless woman, with a necklet of blue beads, a white muslin dress, stockings and saucy sandals.

St Edward Street in the days before the new Post Office was built in the street. The shop of Salter & Salter, boot manufacturers, can be identified at No 32. It is the tall building in the centre of the photograph. A little lower down the street between Nos 34 and 36 was the entrance to Court 6, known as Dale's Yard. The entrance can be identified as the narrow gap between them. Sixteen houses once stood in this court. In 1894 Isaac Booth of Liverpool owned Nos 1 and 2 Dale's Yard and Nos 36 and 40 St Edward Street. The properties seen here were demolished to make way for the new Post Office, which opened in 1964.

In 1881 this house at 54, St. Edward Street was empty, possibly because it was being prepared for the arrival of Thomas and Elizabeth Wardle and family. They had been living at the stone house lower down the street (No 62). Thomas Wardle died at 54, St Edward Street in 1909 and his son, Gilbert, purchased the house that year. The property was sold with "two cottages in the yard and four others". Outside the house were a conservatory, tennis lawn, paddock, stables and a carriage house. The house also served as offices for the Wardle business until 1915. Later, after another change of ownership, Mrs M E Rogers ran a boarding house there. Finally Bowcocks, the solicitors, bought the house and Bowcock and Pursaill still have their offices here.

The Cheshire Cheese stood on the corner of Spout Street (St. Edward Street) and Sheepmarket. The inn advertised large and spacious smoke and commercial rooms in 1904 together with wines and spirits of superior quality. Further up the street was a blacksmith's and the George Hotel can be seen on the top right corner.

3. SHEEPMARKET

Young women pose happily for a photograph in Sheepmarket in VE day on 1945
There were many celebrations in the town with people taking to the streets to sing, dance and party.

4. STANLEY STREET

A snowy scene in Stanley Street, once known as Custard Street. The hanging sign denotes the situation of the Queens Head now renamed " The Valiant". In 1837, George Walker was the landlord here as wall as acting as agent for Cheddleton Brewery. Nearly one hundred years later Thomas Pickford was a barman here. Queens Square, behind the Queens Head contained a house; a warehouse and workshops. These were advertised for sale in 1828.

The Cross Keys Inn in Stanley Street. This was later a site occupied by The Bazaar. Two crossed keys may just be seen on the inn sign.

This cinema started life in 1909 as The Grand Theatre and Hippodrome. It was built by Sampson Salt for a group of local businessmen including Mr Barnfather, a coachbuilder in Haywood street, Harry Davenport, the landlord of the Black Swan and Mr J Ratcliffe who was a plumber in St Edward Street. Barry Bond was the manager of the theatre and put on both local and national acts. At first it was just a theatre but soon began to include silent movies alongside live entertainment. In 1915, after the theatre had been closed for reconstruction, it began to show films only.

Two cinemas were located in High Street; the Grand and the Palace. The canopy in front of the Palace can be seen here in the left foreground. Beginning its life as a roller skating rink on the corner of High street and Salisbury Street it was converted to a cinema by 1911. The cinema was first known as the Salisbury Electric Picture Palace and from the 1920s it became The Palace. By the 1960s it had become The Regal. Later it was used as a bingo hall and then became the Kingdom Hall of the Jehovah's Witnesses. The front of this building has been demolished and replaced by modern apartments.

Here is The Field, better known as Field House in use as a private residence. It is now in High Street, but formerly its grounds stretched to Strangman Street and between Salisbury Street and the rear of the properties fronting St. Edward Street.

This early 19th century house was built for brothers William and Samuel Phillips who were silk manufacturers. After the brothers died, the house was occupied by Thomas and Catherine Whittles and their family. The beginning of the 20th Century saw the grounds of Field House sold for housing. In later years, this house was used as a registration centre for enlistment in World War I. It has been run as a temperance hotel and is now Leek National Reserve club.

6. STOCKWELL STREET

Stockwell Street before the advent of the motor car. Hooves strike on the cobblestones as a cart lumbers up the street towards the Market Place. Carts of all shapes and sizes line the street awaiting goods to transport around the town and to neighbouring villages. The right hand side of the street remains unchanged. Ford House and the gable end of Stockwell Cottage can be seen in the distance.

The old bow window of Haworth's can be seen in this early photograph of a leisurely and leafy Stockwell Street Next to it is 5, Stockwell Street which used to be the home of Miss Mary Hawksworth, a dressmaker and later of Sidney Mountcastle Phillips. This house had a large garden at the rear. On the opposite side of the street, below the gas lamp is 10, Stockwell Street. This large house was originally the home of Thomas Walthall, a lawyer. In the 20th century it has housed members of the Flint family, descendants of Charles Flint, a Leek doctor, who lived here long ago. Mrs Edward Challinor lived here in 1912, but in more recent years it will be recalled as being the dental surgery of Mr. Starkie, the Moorlands Training Centre and Leek College Training Centre.

To the left of the horses in this snowy Stockwell Street scene are Nos 12 and 14, 16 and 18 are just above them. 12 and 14 were for many years were the premises of Joseph Phillips, an ironmonger. Joseph was the son of Edwin Phillips and had started his business at No 12 by 1901. As his business expanded he took over the shop next door at No 14 and traded at these premises also. Before Joseph began his ironmongery business here, Edward Hallowes, a printer and bookbinder, occupied a shop at No 14. Mr Hallowes was remembered as an old man with white whiskers and a beard. He always wore a long dark coat and a white apron; both he and his shop were objects of fascination for young boys who came to buy a pennyworth of slate pencils', sponges, etc. The shop was dark and had interesting glass cases, with sliding doors, containing all manner of things, including a large stock of bibles. It may be that Mr Hallowes shop was in an older building than the one pictured here.

In 1996, 12 Stockwell Street was the home of Bagan Bari Indian takeaway and is now with No 14, Moorlands Pizza and Balti. In recent years HSS Hire Shop traded from 14, Stockwell Street.

11 and 13, Stockwell Street have been demolished for many year, next to them was Court No. 3 containing three houses. This Court was known as Cavendish Square. In this photograph, taken in the 1960s we can see Grosvenor's antiques shop and Fred Spearing, family grocer's. Spearing had been at this shop for many years but in the early 1900s it was occupied by James Fisher, nurseryman and seedsman. 11, Stockwell Street was once the refreshment rooms of Thomas Rendall.

This Georgian House was built between 1750 and 1788 on the site of four cottages. It was the home of Thomas Walthall, a lawyer, who died here in 1788. Charles Flint, a local doctor, lived here before he moved to Compton House. Margaret Smith, a lady of independent means, lived here in 1871 and 1881. This old lady lived alone apart from the three servants who looked after her. In 1912 Mrs Edward Challinor lived here. The house has had alternative uses over the years; a dentist named Starkie practised here and older Leek mothers can remember collecting orange juice cod liver oil and dried milk for their babies. Once part of the Housing and Health department of Staffordshire Moorlands District Council and later used as Leek College's Hair and Beauty Department it is now empty.

The former Stockwell House situated between the old Buiding Society Offices at 15, Stockwell Street and Greystones. This imposing building had a large garden at the rear. It was the home of the Nicholson Family f Brough, Nicholson and Hall, who had moved here from Greystones. Joshua and Ellen Nicholson lived at Stockwell House with their children and servants. By 1932 it was the home of Colonel Arthur Falkner Nicholson. and was demolished before 1936.

Part of the pleasure garden behind the former Stockwell House.

The building at the top of Stockwell Street which was used as Leek's fire station from 1870. This old property was once part of the Cock Inn, which stood on the corner of the Market Place and Stockwell Street. The large house in the centre is 10, Stockwell Street, still in use as a private house. A new town house has recently been built above this property which blends in well with the street scene. The old buildings were replaced by a new fire station which now has a new lease if life as The Engine Room, a drinking and eating establishment.

A cow strolls, slowly, past the entrance to the Nicholson Institute. This Queen Anne style building, of brick with stone dressings, was designed by William Sugden. It was presented to the town by Joshua Nicholson and opened in 1884. The library contained over 6,000 books and was open to all adults living within 6 miles of Leek. The Nicholson Institute also contained a museum and three picture galleries.

The late 17th century Greystones presents a timeless face to both old and modern Stockwell Street. The cottage next to Greystones has long gone as have the cobblestones. The railings on the wall opposite have been replaced with a hedge but little else seems to have changed. Greystones once had a garden at the rear with views over Hillswood and Gun. Sunflowers and hollyhocks blossomed in this quaint garden which was lost when the Nicholson Institute was built. Arthur Nicholson lived at this house before he moved to Highfield Hall. For many years Henry Salt, who was first a cashier and eventually a director of Brough, Nicholson and Hall, lived here. Greystones was, for many years, the award-winning tea rooms of Mr and Mrs Warrilow. It is now their private residence.

Above: Many people will recall when Leek had a museum located in the entrance to the library in the Nicholson Institute. Arranging items in the display case are Edith Jerram, the librarian, and Eileen Allen, a library assistant. After many years display cases can once again be seen in the library with changing displays from the Leek collection.

Left: The Majestic Cinema in Union Street, conjures up happy memories for Leek children, who spent many enjoyable hours inside. The Majestic occupied the former Temperance Hall and opened as a cinema in the early 1920s. It was gutted by fire in 1961 and was demolished soon afterwards.

A crowd of children gathered outside the Majestic Cinema. The boys grin, engagingly at the front, while the girls smile, happily behind them. Whether they were waiting to go in, or had just come out, is not known.

Stockwell Street almost hidden by the mass of people gathered to watch the parade. Here the Boys Brigade take centre stage.

An evocative photograph by Arthur Goldstraw looking towards Park Terrace with the chimney of Clemesha Bros & Birch soaring above the factory. A silk mill on New Street was once worked by Gaunt and Wardle. In the 1830s Gaunt, Wardle and Walmsley were in business here. By 1872 Alsop Downes and Spilsbury occupied New Street Mill and manufactured silk thread there for many years. Alsop, Downes and Spilsbury employed hand loom weavers in the mill in 1900, they made dress fabrics and tailor serges. In 1907 Clemesha's moved into this mill.

Above: Workers streaming out of Clemesha's, one suspects that they knew the photograph was to be taken as they are all dressed in their best! This ornate doorway can still be seen in New Street. Over 500 people worked for Clemesha's in Ariel and New Street Mills.

John Chapman Clemesha, the founder of the firm. Born in Preston in December 1849 and educated at Ackworth boarding school in Yorkshire, he came to Leek in 1873. In 1881 John was lodging at 4 Ball Haye Road and was described as a silk manufacturer employing 6 hands. When Clemesha Bros & Birch celebrated their Jubilee in 1923 John Clemesha was presented with a case of gold mounted Loewe briar pipes.

In 1932 Mrs Lizzie Lees was a hardware dealer at 45, Stockwell Street. Her goods are shown displayed on the pavement as well as in the shop window. She sold a wonderful variety of goods including, brooms, buckets, kettles, baskets, steps, trays, saucepans and crockery! A careful study of the photographs will reveal many more.

James Alsop died in 1868 and his widow Adelina Alsop built the Leek Memorial Cottage Hospital in memory of her husband. The hospital was designed by William Sugden and opened in 1870. When the hospital first opened it had two wards with beds for four men and three women, two cots and two private wards containing one bed each. This photograph was taken before 1909.

Church Street, lavishly adorned with foliage and flags, on a hot summer's day in June 1887. Queen Victoria's Golden Jubilee was celebrated throughout the town with parades, feasts, sports, dancing, fireworks, bonfires and much merriment. Here a group of people are pictured outside the Conservative Club. This Tudor style building was erected in 1887 on the site of the former Crown Inn, which was pulled down in 1886. The Conservative Club, founded in 1882, formerly met in the Union Buildings in Market Street. Opened on 12 April 1887, by Mr Harry Davenport MP, the Conservative Club contained a reading room and a "double American bowling alley". Upstairs were two billiard rooms, two smoking or card rooms and a dining room. The south side of Church Street was demolished in 1972 in order to widen the road and to improve the junction with St. Edward Street.

This arch in Stockwell Street was erected to celebrate the visit of the Duke and Duchess of York on 28th July 1900. This unusual view shows the side of West's shop which faced Stockwell Street. The other side stretched down Church Street opposite the shops and vicarage. Their view of the town was much improved when this property was demolished.

A view of the old, narrow, Church Street circa 1920. Wooden pails and other implements are stacked on the roadway. The houses on the left are 2 and 4 Church Street next to the vicarage. In the years before 1919 Mr Arthur Parker, land agent and surveyor occupied 4, Church Street, which was the estate office of the Earl of Macclesfield. (Thomas Parker, who became the 1st Earl of Macclesfield was born in these premises in 1666). In 1916 George Hardy, an electrician traded from

this property. For many years 4, Church Street has been known as Bill's store, fondly known as "Bill the Bandit".

2, Church Street was converted into two shops, which have changed hands and trades, often, over the years. In 1932 and 1940 John Joseph Curtis was a cabinet maker at number 2. Mrs Cumberlidge has sold hats for many years in the Market Place and the shop next door has seen many tenants having traded as a ladies clothes shop, a music shop and a garden shop, to name but a few.

The Golden Lion Inn at 9 Church Street is still remembered by many Leek people. This old established inn was a busy drinking establishment as long ago as 1829. At that time it boasted a bar and five rooms on the ground floor, a brewhouse and eleven bedrooms. In the large yard behind the Inn had stabling for forty horses and there were five warehouses. One of these warehouses was occupied as a dwelling house and another was used as a slaughter house.

A view of the lower end of Church Street showing the Conservative Club, Cumberlidge's Hat shop and the George Hotel. Yet another place for liquid refreshment can be seen, namely The Swan. Note the absence of the attractive black and white frontage and the pleasant wide pavement, which we see today.

15, Church Street, another old property with a new shop front. For many years this was the millinery shop of Hannah and Sarah Garner. In living memory it has been the confectionery shop of Mr. Granville Wragg, the tobacconist shop of Doris Goodwin and later of Mr. C Bowling. The Conservative Club is on the extreme right of the photograph.

West Street Sunday School Scholars head to the Market Place in 1910 as proud relatives, dressed in their best, line the banks on either side. It seems that the cobbles have been sauced up for this occasion as there is no horse manure to be seen!

Market Day in Leek as drovers and cattle wend their weary way up Mill Street to reach the Cattle Market. The cows, not being conversant with the Highway Code, did not always keep to the road and would often run down entries and become trapped in backyards. Children delighted in the mayhem which followed as the animals were chased back into the road!

The Property on the left has been demolished but the house standing next to it is Bank House or Clerk Bank House which has recently been repainted in an authentic blue shade. Bank House has been home to William Young, Thomas Wardle (not Sir Thomas) and Ralph de Tunstall Sneyd. Doctors Depree and Mansbridge practised here and Norman Smith ran an undertakers business from this property. In recent years it has been home to Inghams Architects and is now the home of Christopher Taylor Design. On the right on Overton Bank is Salt's builder's yard.

Left of the Quaker Cottages is Overton Bank House. Many people will remember this property when it was occupied by John Nokes and Sons, cabinet makers. John Nokes ran his business from the Wilkes Yard before moving to Overton Bank. Next to the Swan is the shop where William Laverack Bullock operated for over 30 years as a cabinet maker, now part of JD's wine bar, it was once an early Co-operative Society shop. This photograph also shows the George and the properties in Church Street which have all been demolished.

On parade. With suitably short hair and forage caps firmly placed, lines of Home Guard members, proceeded by bandsmen, march smartly up Mill Street for a church parade. Crowds of Leek people always gathered to support the local men.

An interesting view of Clerk Bank looking towards West Street with the factory of Stephen Goodwin and Tatton still extant. It was destroyed by fire in the 1940s and remained a ruin for many years. Noticeably absent from this view are the toilets at the top of Mill Street

The building on the extreme left is no longer with us. Situated on Clerk or School Bank, it was once kept by Uriah Davenport in the early 1800s. It was the Beehive pub.

Living in these eight houses in Naylor Yard in the latter part of the 19th century were silk twisters, winders, piecers, spoolers, a charwoman and a shoemaker. Most of the residents were born in Leek but John Cooling, at No 11, came from Ireland. He was a wood turner and had arrived in Leek by way of Manchester, Yorkshire and Liverpool; three of his five children were born in those locations. Businesses were also

carried out in the yard, William Haywood made mineral water in the yard as a sideline to his main employment as landlord of the Golden Lion in Church Street. He abandoned the innkeeping and concentrated solely on the mineral water. He was still in business in Naylor Yard in 1928.

Brow Hill House built in the late 1830s stood between Mill Street and Daisy Bank. The house had three storeys and extensive grounds with greenhouses and a vinery. At one time Robert Hammersley, a partner in the silk dyeing firm at Bridge End, occupied the house and later several generations of the Myatt family lived there. They were silk manufacturers trading from Alexandra Mill. This beautiful house was demolished after 1959 and council housing built on the site.

9. PETTY FRANCE

The enigmatic character of the cottages behind St. Edward's Church is captured in this evocative photograph. Known locally as Petty France the rows of cottages comprised Ball Lane and the courts leading from it. Petty France is thought to be a corruption of Petite France (Little France) and this area was once believed to be the home of all the French Prisoners who lived in Leek in the early 19th century. Recent research has found that most of these houses were not built until after 1808 and that the prisoners were, in fact, lodged all over the town. Perhaps some Frenchmen did lodge here for a short time but the name Petty France is more likely to have arisen because of the close proximity of the lower churchyard where several of the prisoners are buried. The cottages were demolished in the 1960s and another aspect of Leek's history disappeared for ever.

This row of four cottages faced the wall of the church yard. The shop on the corner was a grocers and sweet shop kept by Mrs. Sharratt.

This row of eight terraced cottages was in the court at the bottom of Ball Lane.

Ball Lane leading down to Brough Park with St. Edward's Cottage on the left.

Keith Drury walks briskly over the uneven road surface of Ball Lane, without the burden of his postman's bag.

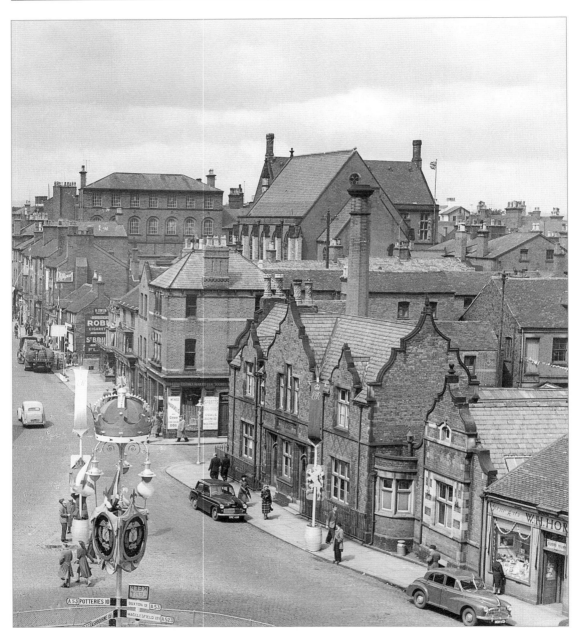

It's 1953 and the town is celebrating Queen Elizabeth's coronation as can be seen by the crown adorning the signpost in the roundabout. Here can be seen Leek's Victorian Public Baths which had a tiled pool and changing rooms with half doors making it rather difficult to preserve one's modesty. The imposing elevations of the Brunswick Chapel, the Central Liberal Club and the Town Hall stand proudly on Market Street. Of the latter only the recently renovated Liberal Club survives.

Derby Street on a busy Wednesday. The cobbled road is lined with carrier's carts and the pavement crowded with shoppers. In 1908 the building on the extreme left was used as offices by the Leek Photographic Society, Samuel Mottram, an auctioneer and valuer, and by Mary Nixon a teacher of music. The double fronted property next door housed John Harry Osbourne's butchers shop and the Dog and Partridge public house. On Wednesday's carriers, carts left the Dog and Partridge for Alstonefield, Warslow and Waterhouses.

The same view on a quieter day. The large house, behind the tree, on the left of the photograph is Gaunt House. The substantial property, once the home of Richard Gaunt, had gardens and pleasure grounds. It was converted into shops now known as Gaunt Buildings.

13, Derby Street. This fine Georgian house was the home and offices of the architects William Sugden and Son. In 1881 William lived here with his wife, four children, a cook and a housemaid. Eventually two shops were built on the garden in front of the house. Today the premises are home to Boots chemists although the top two floors seem to have changed little when viewed from the street.

The Midland Bank with a very interesting car parked outside. Today the bank, built on the site of Magnier's corn merchant's premises, is a branch of HSBC.

A coach laden with baskets stands outside the Cock Inn at 19, Derby Street. The inn has been established here by the early 19th century. In the early years of the 20th century, John Munro operated a wine and spirit business from these premises while his son Murdo Munro was the landlord. John Munro came from Tairn in the Scottish Highlands. He settled in Rudyard, building Fairview there in 1879/80. Later Munro's wine business moved to Stanley Street and was eventually taken over by John Joules brewery of Stone. When Bass bought that brewery, Munros was closed down.

Stanley & Hope Porter [joint author's parents] purchased their first television from Hammersley's shop in Derby Street to watch the Coronation at home. For many with no TV, other arrangements were necessary. Here a group of people watch the state occasion on TVs in the windows of Hammersley's shop. Here a group of people watch the state occasion on TVs in the windows of Hammersley's shop which stood on the left corner of Derby Street and Market Street.

Wendy Walton serving customers on the Save the Children stall in Derby Street at the Pied Poudre event in 1990.

James Hall Tatton, baker and confectioner, traded here from at least 1908. He moved to these premises at 22, Derby Street from another shop on the opposite side of the street which later became the Maypole Stores. J.H. Tatton and Co. was given a false black and white frontage so that it would blend in with the Roebuck Hotel. Many Leek people will remember Tatton's bread with it's distinctive wrappers or recall the ladies who served them coffee and scrumptious cakes. These ladies in their black uniforms with white caps and aprons were required to keep their hair short or fastened up and were not allowed to wear perfume or nail varnish.

The Roebuck was one of Leek's main coaching inns. 'Telegraph' coaches called here on their journeys between London and Manchester. Together with other coaching inns in Leek the Roebuck provided accommodation for travellers and stabling for horses. According to the Victoria County History, before 1848 Russell Street was called Roebuck Lane. However, local tradition in the town differs: Roebuck Lane being the lane to Brook Street which runs down the side of the inn. The Lowndes family sold it for £4,120 in 1876. Messrs Bell and Co of Burton took over the Roebuck in 1882.

Although dated 1626, no records of an inn called the Roebuck exist until the 18th century. Recent research suggests that the inn was originally a private house.

Left middle & bottom: On the photograph (below) the public weighing machine, which formerly stood here, has now been replaced by public conveniences. Note the gas lamps lining each side of the street. On the right is 65 Derby Street, the home of Leek's Public Baths for many years. At one time as many as 200 people used the slipper baths for their weekly ablutions. Patrons would wait in a room for their turn to bathe. Females would be conducted to a bath by the superintendent's wife. She filled the bath for you and turned off the hot tap very tightly to stop you getting more than your fair share of hot water! The bath cost 6d and a towel and bar of soap were provided. When stepping out of the bath it was wise to keep an eye out for cockroaches!

Swimmers had the use of the 60 feet by 20 feet white tiled pool. At first, mixed bathing was not allowed but when it was introduced some years later attendances at the baths soared.

The Baths were demolished in 1975 and a new building now stands on the site which is a branch of the Britannia Building Society.

This early view of Derby Street clearly shows Carding's, grocers and corn dealers. Sacks outside the store are most likely waiting to be loaded onto the cart. It later became Biddulph and District Agricultural Society's premises. The shop opposite Carding's was Goldstraws and has subsequently been rebuilt.

Changing times in Derby Street. Melia's is now Wright's Pie shop while Peak Pharmacy and Dollond and Aitchison occupy the old Moreton's site. The former M.E.B shop is now a charity shop called Scope.

Morton's Yard. A court off Derby Street reached through an entry next to 42, Derby Street. These houses have now been demolished and the yard is no longer accessible.

Houses in Derby Street long since converted to shops. To the left are the arched windows of Bayley's butchers shop. The small house in the centre was supposedly once the home of a Mrs. Bill. The imposing house with six windows was, in 1892, the home of John Brearley. He was born in Leek in 1832 the son of Thomas Brearley, a land agent. By 1871 John Brearley was the senior partner in the Brearley firm of land agents and surveyors. The house on the extreme right was the home, in 1908, of Archibald Somerville M.D. Physician and Surgeon. The conversion from house to shop is recorded in this scene.

The same properties in the 1960's with shops at ground level.

Flags flying to mark a festive occasion in Derby Street. In 1892 the two shops either side of the entrance to Deansgate were, on the left, William Eaton (baker) and on the right, Miss Mary Deane (milliner). A gate used to hang between the properties across Deangate. To the left of Deansgate is a wooden structure. What was its purpose? The glass lantern slide is broken, hence the lines across the photograph.

The double fronted property to the right of the Duke of York was once Birchall's shops. Mr Anos [sic] Birchall was a hairdresser at 55, Derby Street as early as 1868. By 1892, he also occupied the other shop and was trading as a hairdresser and tobacconist. At Birchall's you could choose between three classes of haircut, 1st, 2nd and 3rd. The lather boys would vie to get the 1st class customers as they gave bigger tips!

Old Mr. Birchall would cut the hair of gentlemen and mill owners 'by invitation only'. These special haircuts took place at the rear of the premises and involved a convivial glass of whisky shared between client and hairdresser. After many haircuts Mr. Birchall became overly fond of his whisky and would be locked in a bedroom by his relatives to dry out. Strangely, he did not seem to improve which puzzled his family until they discovered him lowering a basket out of his window. The landlord of the adjoining Duke of York was replenishing his supplies which were quickly hauled up to the bedroom!

A fine team of horses wait patiently for the passengers to board the coach which will take them to Buxton. People crowd the pavement outside the Duke of York waiting to watch the coach move off. The Duke of York was one of Leek's old public houses. In 1804 Mary Lees, daughter of the landlord, married Jacques Francois Neau. Captain Neau was one of the French Napoleonic prisoners of war who were paroled to Leek. Arriving in Leek in December 1803 he had wooed and married Mary within a few months of his arrival!

The fence on the right marks the boundary of the old cattle market at the bottom of Derby Street. The house is Cawdry House, which stood in Fountain Street. After the house was demolished Cawdry Buildings were erected on this site.

This is Getliffe's Yard off Derby Street. The former name of this court was Cope's Yard. Simon Getliffe, a corn merchant, married Ann Cope in 1794 and it can be speculated that this event initiated the change of name. Simon and his family lived in a house in Derby Street at the head of the yard. The Getliffe family still owned the houses in this yard in 1894. In the closing years of the 19th century over 70 people were living in Getliffe's Yard. At this time Rupert Getliffe, the grandson of Simon, owned the houses. Families occupied only 9 or 10 of the houses in the yard, but there were also two lodging houses. The latter were situated at Nos 19, 21, 25 and 27. In each case two houses were used as one lodging house. On the night of the census, in 1891, over 20 men were lodging in Getliffe's Yard. A number of these men were just passing through Leek before travelling on to other towns. They were hawkers, pedlars and knife grinders. Others were carters, ostlers and agricultural labourers who were presumably employed in Leek.

President Kemp's Palace of Light and Music seen here on the site of the old cattle market in Derby Street was a travelling bioscope show. To tempt the townspeople to pay to see the show, Kemp's had dancing girls who performed on a wooden platform erected on the cobblestones. Alice Ralphs remembered watching these dancing girls as a young child, but she never saw the show, as she couldn't afford the entrance fee.

Sanders Buildings built for William Sanders to a Sugden design in 1894. With its oriel window, stone pilasters, decorative urns and domed turret the building embraces the Arts and Craft movement which typifies much of Sugden's architecture. In 1896 the two shops were occupied by Mr. Sanders, who was a florist and seedsman and William Mears who traded as an outfitter. Eventually James Mears, nephew of William Sanders took over the florist business so that the Mears family traded from both these shops. They continued to do so for many years and the building became known locally as Mears' Corner. A closer look at this lively photograph will reveal many details, including cows passing in front of the buildings.

Will they buy or are they just enjoying the patter? This group of men are gathered at the bottom of Derby Street where a cheapjack is touting his wares. Whatever he is selling is obviously of no interest to a lady! Notice the boy with no shoes.

A fine view of Sparrow Park, the name given to the area in front of The Monument in the days before traffic began to roar past the roundabout. It was possible to sit beneath the tree and enjoy the peace and quiet! In the background is the Cattle Market Inn built by Thomas Fernihough in 1867, who also built St. Luke's Church. The Inn gained its pleasing frontages in 1875 when Thomas Brearley enlarged and altered the property, adding moulded bricks, decorative terracotta tiles and carved stonework. The Cattle Market Inn was always popular with both farmers and townsfolk during the hustle and bustle of busy market days.

Here we can see the two-storey building once owned by Beech, the builders, which was Leeks last smithy. The large building was a nicely proportioned textile mill. The three-storey house beyond the smithy has been demolished. It also had a frontage to Cross Street. Peeping out at the end of the properties are the petrol pumps of Hodkinson's Filling station which tragically caught fire in 1969.

A fine photograph of J Meakin's premises in Ashbourne Road. Although the sign identifies him as a wheelwright and carriage builder he also ran a blacksmith's shop.

Building Leek's new Bus Station which was ofically opened in October.

Hodkinson's Filling Station where the petrol pumps were on the edge of the pavement. In August 1969 petrol vapours were ignited by a naked flame on a gas powered refrigerator inside the building. The resulting conflagration ignited the cab of a petrol tanker parked outside on the road. As the intense heat began to blister the paint on the tanker Arthur Allen, a leading fireman, climbed inside the cab of the tanker and released the brake. The tanker was in imminent danger of exploding and at the time burning petrol was running down the street. Mr Hodkinson, who had been pulled from the building by his son David, later died as a result of his injuries. Both Mr Allen and David showed incredible bravery that day.

Above left: Finnikin's Garge in Ashbourne Road before its modern forecourt was constructed. The garage was started by Harry Finnikin and was taken over in the late 1950s by Percy Goodwin , who had married one of Harry Finnikin's daughters. Norman Ainsworth and his wife purchased the garage in 1978 and still run it today. However by the end of this year his daughter and son-in-law will take over the business as Norman plans to retire. Just to the left of this photograph was Court 8 London Road, which features in the Courts and Yards chapter of this book. **Right:** Percy Goodwin who took over Finnikin's Garage in the late 1950s.

Opened in 1880 at 30, London Road, this branch of the Leek and Moorlands Industrial Provident Society Ltd., also provided a bakery. The Society later reverted to it's original name of the Leek and Moorlands Co-operative Society. New central premises designed by Larner Sugden were built here in 1899 as the plaque on the building confirms. The lovely terracotta and cream friezes, bearing the words: "Building; gardening; weaving; Leek Half; mechanic; farming and trade", have recently been restored. Refurbished in 1997, by the Staffordshire Housing Association after falling into disrepair, the building contains 7 flats and has been renamed Penny Bank House.

Employees of Haywood Mills are having a good time at their first dance held in the Co-Operative Hall in 1948.

A Primitive Methodist Chapel was built in Fountain Street in 1836 and rebuilt later in 1884. Two hundred and seventeen people attended the Sunday evening service here in 1851. The congregation moved to the New Connection Chapel at the corner of Ball Haye Street and Queen Street in 1949. The old chapel was used for various purposes over the years, once being offices for the Inland Revenue. The former Primitive Methodist Chapel was demolished in the early 1970s.

Fountain Street festooned with bunting to celebrate a royal visit. Cawdry Buildings are to the right and the Fountain Street Chapel is to the left.

Left & p62 top: This property adjacent to the Fountain Inn in Fountain Street was demolished to make way for Leek's new Police Station. The Fountain is another of Leek's old inns having been established on this site from at least 1837. Fountain Street probably stands on the site of an old medieval road; the present street takes its name from the reservoir, dating from the 18th century. This used to be at the eastern end of the street bounded also by The Organ Ground and East Street. A new housing estate now stands on the site of this old reservoir.

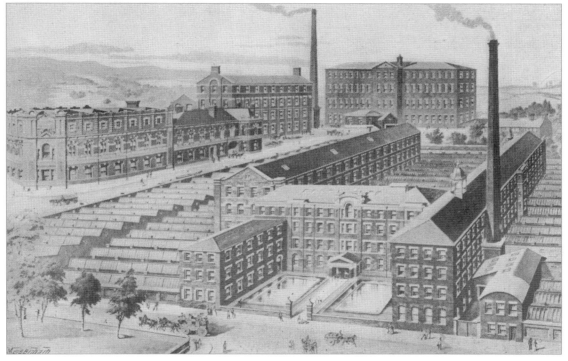

The ponds in front of Hope Mill, in Fountain Street, can be clearly seen in this stylised drawing. The Brough, Nicholson and Hall complex was able to treat the raw silk and process it until it reached the finished product. The mills had their own joinery, box and printing shops. During the wars, Broughs played a part in supplying the armed forces. They made miles of parachute cord, medal ribbons and webbing.

Hope Mill in Fountain Street was established by Thomas Carr in the 1820s. In 1851, when Mr Carr was manufacturing silk thread here, there was a fish pond, stocked with 600 goldfish, in front of Hope Mill. The pond was enclosed with palisades and supplied with fresh water from the engine pump. Many Leek people will remember Hope Mill when it was owned by Brough Nicholson and Hall; it had two ponds in front of it even then. Hope Mill and the buildings on the west side of Cross Street were demolished in 1968. The Health Centre now occupies this site

Fountain Mill was situated on the corner of Fountain Street and Well Street. The police station now occupies this site. Broughs took over the mill from Messrs George H Bermingham & Co. In 1907 Broughs installed machinery in Fountain Mill for the production of spun silk.

Above left: A Morris 1000 van is parked on the cobbles of Fountain Street outside Hope Mill. Above Hope Mill is Concrete Mill, then the Fountain Inn and houses which were once rented to employees of Brough, Nicholson and Hall. On the extreme edge of the photograph is Fountain Mill. In 1966 Broughs specialised in braids, braided cords, lacing and crepe cords, braided ties, fancy trimmings, gymnasium girdles, wilting cords, boot, shoe and corset laces, embroidered badges, woven labels, ribbons, seam bindings, petershams, shoulder strappings, hat bands, blazer bindings and regalia ribbons!

Above right: Looking down Fountain Street with Concrete Mill beyond the Fountain Inn. The vast Brough, Nicholson and Hall site between Fountain Street and Cross Street was demolished in the late 1960s. The Health Centre, the Social Services building and the Police Station now stand on the site once occupied by the buildings depicted here. The Fountain Inn is the sole survivor.

In 1892 Isabella Carr erected these almshouses, at a cost of £4,000, on the corner of Fountain Street and Osbourne Street. They were built in memory of her sisters Rosanna and Ellen, who died in 1858 and 1888 respectively. The almshouses were endowed by Isabella, each inmate receiving a shilling a day. Originally they were for 3 aged females of Leek who had been in domestic service, but the criteria changed so that men or women who were members of the Church of England could live there.

12. PICKWOOD ROAD

This narrow cobbled passageway connected Derby Street to Brook Street. It started life as Black-a-moor's Head Lane before becoming known as Backsides. Understandably the inhabitants were not overly impressed by this name and asked William Challinor if the name could be changed to Pickwood Road. The following pages comprise a unique photographic record of the houses which once stood in this part of old Leek.

The poster advertising the "News of the World" marks the site of Bloore's wholesale newspaper business. In the days when newsagents were closed on Sundays many people made their way to Pickwood Road to buy their paper from Mr. Bloore. Men and boys would trundle along to the building with little carts which they filled with newspapers to sell around the town.

Small terraced houses with few rooms lined Pickwood Road. The occupants of these houses could easily look over a wall to the large gardens of houses in St. Edward Street. There, ladies would be taking their leisure or indulging in a game of tennis. A marked contrast to the way of life of people who lived in Pickwood Road.

This factory was situated at the bottom of Pickwood Road. The houses and premises in Pickwood Road were demolished in 1984 to make way for the new Normid Superstore and its car park. The line of Pickwood Road still remains connecting Brook Street with Derby Street.

13. MARKET STREET

Looking down the length of Market Street with Ford House in the left foreground. The garden to the side was originally much larger but was sold off for building land. Nearby Ford Street was built on part of this land. Further along the same side of the street is Brunswick Chapel and on the right hand side is the Town Hall. Both of these properties have been demolished.

Ford House stands at the corner of Market Street and Stockwell Street. Occupied today by Fearns Marriot, accountants, it was originally the home of Hugh Ford. Hugh Ford (1750-1797) was a descendant of the Ford family from Ford Green Hall, who were Quakers. He settled in Leek as a silk button merchant and built this house. After his death his son, also Hugh, lived here.

By 1841 Francis Cruso, brother of John Cruso from the house we now call Foxlowe, lived here. Francis Cruso was a lawyer, he was also the town's Superintendent Registrar as well as serving as clerk to local magistrates and to the Board of Guardians. In 1851 Francis employed a governess, cook, housemaid, kitchen maid and a man servant to look after the needs of himself and his 15 year old daughter, Jane.

Jane Cruso married William Beamont Badnall in 1854 and they were living here in 1861. Ford House was offered for sale in 1861 together with 2,540 square yards of land. The house had dining and drawing rooms, a library, kitchen, scullery, two cellars, six bedrooms and two dressing rooms. Outside were two coach houses, stabling for two horses, a harness room, pleasure grounds and a croft. The house changed hands

The office and printing works of the *Leek Times* in Market Street, formerly the silk factory of Messrs Fynney & Co.

The former Fynney's mill and Miller's printing works is now Leek Central Club. The only significant change to the exterior is the addition of the large oriel window. Larner Sugden had been given the job of altering the building. When the premises opened, in 1898, the Leek Times described it as the club house of the Leek Division Liberals and Radicals. Inside were reading rooms, offices, a skittle alley, smokeroom and billiard room. The interior decorations were very colourful with chrome yellow or red lacquered walls, dark walnut woodwork and peacock blue seats.

Looking over at the Town Hall from the site of the demolished Brunswick Chapel. This area is now a neatly laid out car park. The Town Hall started life in 1878 as Union Buildings which was built as a concert hall. Leek Improvement Commissioners purchased these premises in 1881 and the building became the Town Hall. Serving both as the headquarters of the town council and as a venue for leisure and cultural activities in Leek, it provided a service which has not yet been replaced. The Staffordshire Moorlands District Council now operates from new premises off Stockwell Street but the dances, concerts and amateur dramatic performances staged in the large concert hall have not found a satisfactory replacement.

The Town Hall surrounded by scaffolding and with most of its roof gone as it is demolished in 1988.

The Town Hall in Leek is packed with children who are attending a party to celebrate VJ Day. The children all have parents who served as soldiers, sailors or airmen during the war. Mrs HCT Hill had organised the party after money had been collected in local public houses and donations given by Leek residents.

The finale of the 1968 Scout Show where the entire cast traditionally sings "We're riding along on the crest of a wave", although quite often the boys would mischievously change the last few words to "the chest of a slave"!

The cast and crew of Camelot, assembled outside the Town Hall in 1987. This was the last show staged in the Town Hall before it was demolished in 1988. Ian Wilson was the producer, as well as taking the role of Arthur, Jean Pointon played Guinevere and Ian Brereton portrayed Lancelot. This successful production, with spectacular costumes and splendid scenery, marked the end of All Saints' lavish, large scale musicals.. Among those pictured here are Ian Wilson, Marilyn Rushton, Michael Birch, Jo Walton, Sophie Pearce, Alice and Harold Rushton and Roger Orme.

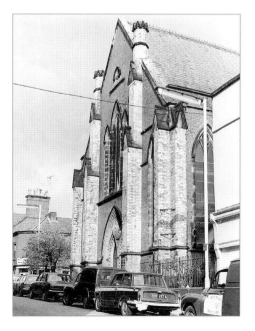

The magnificent gothic-style Brunswick Chapel which stood opposite the Town Hall in Market Street. Built by John Matthews of brick with stone dressings and designed by William Sugden.

The cost of building this soaring edifice in 1856 was £4,381. It was the gift of James Wardle. Further improvements were made to the chapel in 1890 at a cost of £1,263.

Regarded as the centre of Methodism in Leek it was found to be structurally unstable resulting in its closure in 1976. Brunswick Chapel was demolished in 1977 and the site of this imposing chapel is now merely a humble car park.

14. BALL HAYE STREET

The Wesleyan School at the corner of Ball Haye Street and Regent Street was built in 1828. Originally intended to be a Sunday school it was also used for services after James Wardle paid for a gallery and an organ. In 1851, 296 people made up the Sunday evening congregation.

Known at first as Brunswick Chapel it was superseded by a chapel of the same name in Market Street. However, the building remained in use as a school until 1914, the pupils transferring to the new County Primary School in East Street. After this date the premises were used for Sunday school classes, church meetings, clinics and as a British Restaurant during World War II. The Leekensians held some of their early productions here and the Magistrates Court operated from here before moving to High Street. In recent years the old schoolrooms and chapel were sold for redevelopment and like its namesake in Market Street, its site is now a car park.

This Georgian House at 31 Ball Haye Street has been associated with the medical profession for many years. It was the residence of Leek's medical officers and in later years the home and surgery of Leek doctor's. The last doctor to live and work here was Stewart McCallum. The house has been renovated and converted into pleasant apartments known as Stockwell Mews.

Another unusual, but well known vehicle, was Mr Bestwick's coal-fired steam car! It was painted blue and it was said that its whistle was from the Flying Dutchman loco. It certainly made an impression when it was used on the streets. We understand it was built by Mr Bestwick and sold after his death. Here the car is parked outside his shop in Ball Haye Street.

This elegant house at the corner of Ball Haye Street and Queen Street was once the home of Robert Wright, a silk manufacturer. It is now the shop and workshop of Smith, Bainbridge & Wardle.

15. QUEEN STREET

In 1856 a society of New Connection Methodists was formed in Leek. Robert Scrivener of Hanley designed this chapel in 1862 for them. It stood at the corner of Queen Street and Ball Haye Street becoming known as Bethesda Chapel by 1875. Ministers of this chapel lived in the two houses attached to the chapel at the bottom of Queen Street. In 1881 at 8, Queen Street lived Thomas Smith a New Connection Minister with his wife Ann and their daughter Jane. They had obviously moved around the country as Thomas was born in Dudley, his wife in Boston, Lincolnshire and their daughter in North Shields, Northumberland.

Although the chapel was closed in the early 1940s it was later used by the Primitive Methodists from Fountain Street. Bethesda Chapel was finally closed in 1963 and after being used for commercial purposes fell into a state of disrepair. The building was demolished in the late 1980s. These two photographs were taken in Queen Street as the old chapel was being demolished.

The Sugden houses in Queen Street designed by Larner Sugden. The house at no 29 was for Larner's own use and a plaque on the house bears the initials WLS and JMBS and the date 1877. The initials refer to William Larner Sugden and his French born wife Josephine Marie Bucquoy Sugden. They had married in 1875 and were living in their new home in 1881. The Sugden houses were built on a plot of land belonging to the cottage at 27 Queen Street owned by Jacques Francois Mien. He was one of the French prisoners on parole in Leek, who had married a Leek girl and settled in the town.

These houses are typical of Larner's 'Queen Ann' style, which has been described as "sweetness and light". Here flowers seem to march along under the bedroom windows, adorn the chimneystacks or delicately enhance the frontage. The doorways have stone surrounds and there are decorative bargeboards, roof and ridge tiles. A careful study will reveal stone heads gazing over the street, coloured glass and brickwork. A house which reveals new details each time it is viewed.

People wait patiently in the bus shelter while young lads linger to look at the cows. Buses to Cheddleton and the Potteries would often be lined up along Haywood Street to collect their passengers before Leek had a purpose built bus station. This photograph also shows the Talbot Hotel, the Smithfield Commercial Restaurant, and Smithfield Cottages. The Smithfield Restaurant was once the Coffee Tavern which was opened on 12 November 1878, by supporters of the Temperance cause. Their aim was to provide a venue where friends could meet for social recreation instead of frequenting public houses. Working men could bring meals in free of charge rather than eat sitting on the curbstones. Tea, coffee and cocoa were provided before work and soup was available every day at 12 noon. There was a reading room and a place to smoke tobacco and a 'settling room' made available each Wednesday where farmers could sort out their business.

The cattle market with the shops of Haywood Street in the background. The Co-op sign hangs from the building which recently housed Autospares but is now Gee's Ironmongers at 63 to 67 Haywood Street. The Co-op shop at 67 was once a hairdressers. Sam Braddock's tonsorial establishment was situated

here in the early years of this century followed by James Sigley who also cut hair. By 1932 Edward Grainger, a china dealer had taken over the shop. Eliza Brough's dining rooms once occupied 65, Haywood Street. Tomlinson and Grindey's signboard can be seen over the door of the shop which is now Photoprint. In the early 1900s this was the Telephone Call Office.

On the extreme left of this picture is UFS large walk round store. In 1960, when this photograph was taken, you could buy a 3 piece suite from them for £38.7.6d and an all wool deep pile hearth rug for £2.7.3d. The Co-op electrical showrooms can be seen as can the offices of the Leek Post at 79, Haywood Street. These offices were once part of Genie's but now houses a Thai Restaurant. Reginald Pointon, a butcher, was at no. 75 in 1912 and Gertrude Broster traded here as a milliner in 1932. Leek Cycle Co. sold bicycles at 81, Haywood Street in the first decade of this century. The former Carriage Restaurant, now Scorpio's take-away, was once home to Marquis Adolphus Cope, a wood carver. George Gunia's jewellers shop was for many years a saddlers shop run by John Henry Shaw.

Clearing up after a busy day in the Cattle Market on Haywood Street.

Crossing Cromwell Terrace, a boy with a bicycle and an older gentleman stop to watch the action at the fair. No prizes for guessing which one was looking forward with anticipation and which one was reflecting on the foolhardiness of the people about to climb on to the Meteorite!

Michael Collins's transport, carrying the fair rides, parked on the Cattle Market site in Haywood Street. The sweet shop and toilets are no longer with us and although Sugden's scottish baronial style Police Station building still survives, it is no longer used by the forces of law and order.

Another view of the crowded fair on the site of the Cattle Market in Haywood Street.

The Cattle Market where the May and November Fairs were held before transferring to the site of the new Smithfield in Junction Road. In the foreground a woman pushes a pram laden with two children past the bus shelter. The Coffee Tavern and Smithfield Cottages, seen here, have long since disappeared from the Leek street scene.

The Coffee Tavern with Smithfield Cottages to the rear. Opened in 1878, The Coffee Tavern was supported by the Temperance Society to encourage the working classes to abstain from alcohol. It provided a venue where people could eat without the opportunity to purchase alcoholic beverages! In later years the Smithfield Commercial Restaurant operated from these premises. Many people will remember the Sharpe family who ran this establishment.

The Cattle Market is no more, weeds have taken hold in the cobbles and the Coffee Tavern is being demolished. The tall chimney at Brough, Nicholson and Hall's factory no longer exists and the Talbot Hotel is no longer open for business and today presents a sorry sight with it's boarded up windows.

Houses which made up Smithfield Terrace. The new Cattle Market or Smithfield in Haywood Street gave it's name to this row of houses. On the 1881 census they are enumerated as 1 to 8 Alsop's Row although there appears to be only seven houses. Mr Alsop's factory, which stood nearby, later became the Coffee Tavern.

A view from the Cattle Market looking towards The Coffee Tavern and the rear of the houses which later became known as Smithfield Terrace.

Smithfield House was built on the corner of Haywood Street and Leonard Street in 1897 for Arthur Noble. In July a banquet at the Town Hall, attended by 80 friends, was held to celebrate the opening. Arthur Noble & Son traded as jewellers and furniture brokers at Smithfield House which was also the Noble family home. In 1901 Arthur, his wife, and their seven children lived here. Just a few years earlier, in 1881, Arthur Noble was a silk twister living with his wife and three young children in Gladstone Street. As Arthur Noble is listed in an 1892 directory, trading at 16-18 Haywood Street, it can be conjectured that Smithfield House replaced an older building. After he died in 1932, aged 81, J Oakes Ash & Son, auctioneers and valuers, occupied Smithfield House. Several of their sales notices can be seen on the windows in this photograph.

Children play happily with hoops on the pavement of Leonard Street. Carts line the street on the left and a quiet and tranquil atmosphere prevails. The house on the left is 10, Leonard Street where Robert Hill had a veterinary practice, the archway has a horses head on top. The next arch, a little further down the street, still has the bottles over it denoting the premises of Richard Massey, ginger beer manufacturer. 'Pop' Massey's cart can be seen outside his factory. The streets in this area of town were named after the owner of the land on which they were built, he was Mr. Leonard Haywood Shoobridge.

Right: Sugden's Scottish Baronial style police station was built in 1891/2. The turrets, crow-stepped chimneys, arched windows and substantial stonework combine to create a powerful and commanding presence. The authoritative architecture is entirely fitting for its purpose. This police station replaced the one built in 1848 at the corner of Mill Street and West Street.

18. LONDON STREET

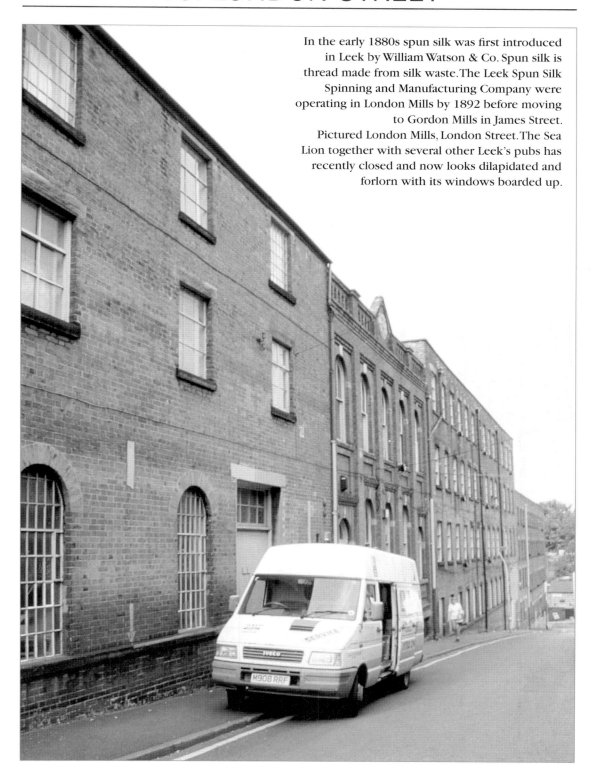

In the early 1880s spun silk was first introduced in Leek by William Watson & Co. Spun silk is thread made from silk waste. The Leek Spun Silk Spinning and Manufacturing Company were operating in London Mills by 1892 before moving to Gordon Mills in James Street. Pictured London Mills, London Street. The Sea Lion together with several other Leek's pubs has recently closed and now looks dilapidated and forlorn with its windows boarded up.

19. SHOOBRIDGE STREET

Hugh Sleigh & Co occupied the mill on the corner of Shoobridge Street and Brook Street from the second half of the 19th century until the 1940s. Hugh Sleigh was a sewing silk manufacturer who lived in St Edward Street. As with other Leek mills this one was used by other businesses over the years. Gwynne & Co eventually bought Hugh Sleigh's mill and at one time Mason's took over the top floor. This building is now used as an antique and interior furnishings shop called 'Haywood Interiors'.

20. RUSSELL STREET

The Sea Lion was established between the years 1838 and 1888. In the late 19th and early 20th centurys, this public house was one of three licensed to John Benson. Herbert Moreton and Daniel Higson were two of the landlords of the Sea Lion in the first half of the 20th century. However, keen observers will note that the Sea Lion has grown! There are now two sets of windows below the door as an extension has been added. Unfortunately the windows are now boarded up as the pub has closed.

Overfield's Furniture Warehouse. This imposing glass fronted building was extended to the design of Larner Sugden in 1896. The impressive, predominant pediment is supported on a framework of single storey columns. The space between the framework is filled with windows with bays in the central spaces. In 1910, Overfield's business was described as "one of the most complete furnishing establishments in North Staffordshire".

Alfred Overfield was born in Shifnal but, by 1851, had moved to Leek trading in Sheep Market and Queen Street before moving to Russell Street by 1854. Alfred died in 1910, aged 86, but the firm of Overfield & Co was still operating in Russell Street in 1921.

10th Leek (Brunswick) Scouts parade down Brook Street with leader Norman Morris on Club Day, ahead of the Brunswick Methodist Sunday School banner. The houses to the left of the parade have all been demolished.

The Leek Post and Times operated from the former workhouse in Brook Street from 1968 before moving to new offices in the Smithfield Centre.

The building is still known as Newspaper House but is now a shop selling beds and bedroom furniture.

This building was formerly a workhouse and later Clowes' dyehouse. Built in 1768, in Spout Lane, it gave its name to Workhouse Street which in turn became Brook Street. The workhouse was enlarged so that by 1834, it was four-storeys high. At this time it had about 54 inmates who were fed and clothed for 3/6d each a week. The children were employed in the Leek silk mills. A new workhouse was built on Ashbourne Road in 1839 (often referred to as "251") and became the Moorlands Hospital in 1948. Prior to 1768, the workhouse was in the building used by Morton's jewellers in Derby Street, prior to its demolition in 1965.

22. WHO DO YOU THINK THEY ARE?

The Arts Club Ball at the Town Hall in 1957.

12th Leek Group
Brownies dressed for
the carnival in the
1970s.

Leek Youth Clubs' Swimming Gala 1958.

2nd Leek Scout Group 1993.

St Mary's Guides.
Guess the year?

Below: The end or the beginning of a journey, Leek Railway Station.

Lux Lux designers in 1976.

The Moonglows, a local 1960s pop group.

INDEX